Take your barbering career to the next level.

CLASSIC BARBER STRATEGY

"The Art of Fade"

By:

TUMELO PATRICK MAHLATSI

[EZEKIEL 5:1]
King James Version

"And thou, son of man, take thee a sharp knife, take thee a barber's razor, and cause *it* to pass upon thine head and upon thy beard: then take thee balances to weigh, and divide the *hair*."

CLASSIC BARBER STRATEGY:
"The art of fade"

Mr. Tumelo Patrick Mahlatsi, Founder of the
Barber Classic Cuts (PTY) Ltd.

Contact:
Tell: +(27)12-065-4239
Email: info@shopbarberclassiccuts.co.za
Website: https://www.shopbarberclassiccuts.co.za/
Social Media:
WhatsApp: +(27)73-972-5319
Facebook: Barber Classic Cuts
Instagram: barber_classic_cuts

Published by: Barber Classic Cuts (Pty) Ltd.
Cover design by: Martin Conduah
Proofreading & editing by: Tumelo Patrick Mahlatsi

Paperback edition ISBN: 978-0-6397-5975-3
NLSA – (National Library of South Africa)
2020

CONTENTS

DEDICATION

This book is dedicated to barbers both beginner and professional who are pursuing entrepreneurship and would love to start their own barbershop or salon business. The book is intended to help you take the first steps in setting up your own barbershop business. Also help you create a profitable barbershop business, capable of earning you a good living and make your dreams come true. This book contains all the necessary information you might need about barbering industry which includes techniques, knowledge, skill, insight, and issues surrounding the barbershop industry. The author, Mr TP Mahlatsi shares the blueprint of his success in opening a brand barbershop business called, "Barber Classic Cuts", and he believes by sharing his personal experience, the process it took, and the journey of his failures and successes will help the reader not to make the same mistakes he made and the journey that took him long time can take the reader a short time. He guarantees that the reader will obtain even more results following this book.

ABOUT THE AUTHOR

Mr. Tumelo Patrick Mahlatsi is an entrepreneur and author of a best-selling book, "Classic Barber Strategy". He is the founder of a brand barbershop business called "Barber Classic Cuts" (Pty)Ltd. Mr Tumelo known as "Classic Barber" was born in the city of Kroonstad, in Free State province. He studied "Computer Science" at Vaal university of technology. Has always dreamed of owning his own brand barbershop business.

Mr. Tumelo grew up cutting the hair of many kids in the neighbourhood from the age of 10-year-old, he was a barbershop owner assistance during school holidays and weekends. Mr Tumelo was raised by a single parent and has 4 siblings. Growing up was challenging due to poverty background at home. He decided to focus on education so he can get a good job and help at home but his dream of owning a barbershop could not be forgotten. He was faced with a financial challenge at the university that lead him back to his dream. He solved his financial challenges by using the gift God gave him of cutting hair, turning the work into a brand business.

Mr Tumelo has acquired many invaluable skills and knowledge regarding hair cutting and the overall industry. Mr TP Mahlatsi has acquired knowledge about the barbering industry, trends, insight and how to manage and run a successful barbershop business. At some point Tumelo was required to fulfil important management roles as well as to provide haircuts in some of the barbershops he worked for to gain experience. Some of Tumelo's personal and professional highlights include:

☐ Has attended various hair cutting training and seminars to maintain touch with specialized techniques and issues surrounding the industry.

☐ Has over +18 years of hair cutting experience.

☐ Has provided haircuts for many well-known individuals.

☐ Has held various middle management duties and roles under various employers.

☐ Is knowledgeable of various traditional and new styles of men's haircuts.

☐ Is very approachable and has honed his people skills.

As indicated above, Tumelo has many great attributes and skills, which he will bring to his business in order to ensure its success. Moreover, he has invested almost half of his life providing great hair cutting services to many satisfied customers. Skills include Marketing skill, management skill, sales skill, leadership skill, communications skill, computer skill, graphic design skill, accounting skill, problem-solving skill, and Entrepreneur skill.

For more information about Mr TP Mahlatsi and his barbershop business visit the website below:

www.shopbarberclassiccuts.co.za

ACKNOWLEDGEMENTS

It would be difficult for me to single out an individual as there are so many bodies that played a huge role in the success of this book. I am afraid therefore that if I mention their names, I may not list them all, I would someone out. Therefore, just allow me to give thanks to the AL-mighty God for everyone who had played a part both in my spiritual and physical life. However, in the elite category that demands mentions are the following persons: My barber friend, Mr Benny Jensen – you played a big role in pushing me to finish this artwork and I appreciate you for all the support you gave me and encouragement throughout difficult times of my business. I have also learned a lot from the business seminars (BARS) hosted by Apostle Miz Mzwakhe Tancredi and I am grateful for prayers, prophecies, guidance I have received from him and not forgetting my best friend Apostle Sive Mateta for the prayers we made for the success of this book and for seeing the best in me. A special thanks to my family - my mother, Miss Elizabeth, and my 4 siblings: Moeketsi, Aupa, Thabo, and Selina.

CLASSIC BARBER STRATEGY
TABLE OF CONTENTS

INTRODUCTION

The barbering/haircut industry it is a fast-growing industry worldwide. The industry is well known for male grooming services such as haircuts, shaves, and hairstyling. I believe our current and next coming youth generation should take advantage of this amazing and exciting opportunity in the barbering career. The barbershop business is improving and growing in most parts of the world.

Most independent barbershop owners today began in the business by working for someone else's shop and felt they could succeed on their own. The barbering industry is wide and full of variety of opportunities to offer, for example small business get an opportunity of partnering with big companies in the industry like "Whal", "Andis", "BaByliss", etc. This manufacturing companies produce barbering products and allow partnership with barbershops to make money from selling their products or become a supplier. I think this is an interesting opportunity each barber should take advantage of and grow their barbershop income. Starting a barbershop business, it's both exciting and challenging journey which can completely change your life and leave you a legacy.

CHARPTER #1:

"INTRODUCTION TO BARBERSHOP INDUSTRY"

1.1. DEFINITION OF THE BARBERING INDUSTRY

The Barber Shop industry is comprised of establishments engaged in providing men's haircuts, shaves, and hairstyling services.

1.2. BARBERSHOP INDUSTRY IN SOUTH AFRICA

THE BARBERSHOP BUSINESS ROLE IN THE COMMUNITY

Barbershops are part of the service-producing industries playing a dominant role in the national economy and collectively account for over two-thirds of the employment generated in South Africa. Barbershops are primarily engaged in providing men's haircuts, hairstyling, hair colouring/dye, face shaving, hair wash and rinse services. The fact that most South African barbershops are small independent operations. Most of these independent operators began in the business by working for someone else's shop and felt they could succeed on their own. Many of these barbershop businesses across the country, is a result of the relative ease and low cost of business start-up and has led to intense competition between barber and salon/beauty shops.

Barbershop industry in South Africa is performing well and achieving moderate growth annually in the service industry. Going into a small business comes with great advantages and opportunities as the government supports small businesses. The improvement of the country's economy depends on the growth or increase in number of small businesses being established in our communities.

SOUTH AFRICAN BARBERSHOP BUSINESSES

The barbershop businesses in south Africa are growing and performing well. Just to mention few of the well-known brands barbershop businesses in South Africa. We have, "Legends barbershop", "Sorbet-man barbershop", "The Famous barbershop", "Thulz barbershop", "Slaqa barbershop", "Rough cuts barbershop", "The shop barbershop, "Barber classic cuts barbershop", "The quality barbershop" and many more.

Barbershops or Salon/Beauty shops that are brand businesses are able to run or operate under a system that can be replicated, which allows their businesses to expand to different areas and still function the same. This business model is known as, "Franchise" which is the best way of building a legacy for a business and improving the economy of the country by creating more jobs. Brand barbershop businesses are the future of our country as it contributes to our community development by providing not only jobs but also skill.

WHY BARBERSHOP BUSINESSES FAIL IN SOUTH AFRICA?

There are many contributing factors to the reason why some barbershop businesses fail, allow me to share some key factors with you:

- **Lack of Vison**
  When you do business without a vision, the business will not have purpose and meaning. Do business based on the gift God has given you, that business will connect with you at your heart level. You can never be fulfilled unless you operate in your gift, your gift is your domain.
- **Lack of focus**
  Focus is staying in one course till it succeed. Don't diversify at an incubation stage of your business.

Don't be jack of all trades and master of none. Wisdom is knowing what not to do, not everything that everyone is doing you should do. For you to focus you must have the ability to say "NO!". You cannot do something with all your heart if your heart is divided, channel your heart on one thing until it succeeds.

- **Lack of endurance**
The real test of faith is the ability to be patient through the process. Business is not a shortcut to success, if you jump up you will come back down but if you grow up you will remain up. Many give up too soon for they expect to sow today and reap tomorrow. Great business takes time to build. Stay in the race till the finish line.

- **Lack of identity**
Copying others is one of the signs you have not discovered your identity. You see someone succeed in a business and you want to start the same business they are doing, that's a recipe for disaster. You must be different from

others and do thing your way and your style. You owe the world YOU! And not you appear like another.

- **Lack of money management**
  You must be very discipline in your finances, knowing the difference between your business bank account and personal bank account. Don't mix personal affairs with business affairs. Your beginning years in your business are you reinvesting years back into the business. Do your calculations and determine the payback period. Your expenses must not exceed your income. Do a bookkeeping.
- **Lack of time discipline**
  Every business owner starts as employee in their business. Commit to your working hours, it doesn't mean if there's no one above you then you should do as you please. Whoever interferes with your time, interferes with your success. Respect time in business and demand that your family and friends do the same.

BARBERSHOP BUSINESS STATISTICS

In most of the brand barbershop businesses we have discovered the following statistics that in some of these barbershops:

- 86% of sales are generated by services with 14% resulting from merchandise sales.
- Approximately 77% of employees are full-time with 23% part-time.
- The revenue of most of these barbershop businesses keeps rising by 7.5% and it hasn't taken a corresponding leap.
- Revenue in these barbershop businesses has dropped marginally for a very long period.
- Conclusion from the gathered statistics suggest that this industry has put up great performance statistics in terms of sales to assets.

BARBERSHOPS IN OTHER COUNTRIES

The barbershop business and the barbering industry is growing and improving all over the world. There's a history behind barbering industry and the United States of America, as they are the leading country in this industry, and they set standards. For examples, in USA, becoming a barber you must have a license and if you want to start a barbershop business you must obtain barbershop permit from the state cosmetology board or licensing department which comes with certain requirements and fees involved for obtaining a barbershop permit which will authorise you to run a barbershop business in the country. There are different types of licenses depending on how you would love to run your barbershop business. Most brand barbershop businesses must obtain the "master barber license" which allows them to expand and have many businesses under one brand.

CHANGES IN THE BARBERSHOP INDUSTRY

One of the major changes that happened with time in barbering industry was when the female barbers started to rise. It was unusual but it became a norm. In America there are many female barbers who have established their own barbershop businesses. The barbering industry is no longer a career dominated by males. This change in the industry has created an exciting competition and growth. Due to this change, today we have haircuts that are specifically designed to accommodate women and it has created a high demand of woman today who prefer haircuts.

1.3. KEY TRENDS AND CHARACTERISTICS OF THE BARBERSHOP INDUSTRY

The following industry characteristics and trends were extracted from various industry publications of South Africa and reports.

- o The barber and beauty shop industry has been growing gradually at an annual 4% over consecutive years till today.

- Many traditional barbers are successfully attending training to learn new contemporary cuts demanded by various demographic segments.
- The average price for a general haircut in South Africa is R50, and for contemporary new haircut styles range from R100 to R250 or more depending on value-added services (includes barber shops only).
- Therefore, the average haircut price is minimum of R50 in the suburbs and R100 in the city.
- Statistics suggests that youths averaged 24–48 haircuts per year while male adults and seniors average 48 annually.
- Barbershops and barbers who operate full-time have and maintain a solid clientele.
- Approximately 75% of a barbershop's clientele are repeat customers.
- Approximately 5% of a shop's customers request shaving or shampooing services.

- In South Africa, the average income for workers in this industry range from the minimum of R4000 as basic salary per month.
- Many barbershops prefer paying their employees based on commission system which is calculated by common rates of 40% by 60% income share, whereby 40% of the income goes to the employee and the business takes 60% of the income.
- Most barbershop business occurs without an appointment, which allows walk-ins.

CHARPTER #2:

"BARBERING SERVICES & HAIR PRODUCTS"

2.1. BARBERING SERVICES

The barbershop business provides professional barbering services which include general & contemporary haircuts, shaves, hair wash & rinse, hair dye/colour, line-up & edges, hair styling and many more.

GENERAL HAIRCUTS

This type of haircut is well known as traditional haircuts. There just two popular traditional haircuts styles which are brush cut and bald cut. These kinds of haircuts they take approximately 15-20 min. Skill is not necessary to perform this haircut all you need is to know how to remove hair.

CONTEMPORARY HAIRCUT

These are new modern haircut styles commonly known as fade haircuts with a touch of hair fibre and hold spray to enhance the haircut. There are approximately more than +10 different haircut styles for this category, which among these the most popular include the Mohawk cut, fade cut, tapper fade and many more. The fade haircut should approximately take 30 minutes.

FACE/BEARD SHAVE & MOUSTACHE

This is done by applying a house face cream and shaving where desired by a customer with a straight blade. It requires experiences using, maintaining, and sharpening a straight blade razor. This type of razor must be used as it is the most effective method. The average shave takes about 10 minutes. After the shave provide customers with a hot cloth and aftershave lotion.

HAIR WASH & RINSE

Hair washing and rinsing prior to or after cuts and or shaves. A house shampoo and conditioner for this service must be offered to all customers. It is estimated that this service takes 7 - 10 minutes in duration. All towels for drying must be provided.

HAIR COLOUR/DYE

There are various types of hair dye colours like black, grey, blonde, blue, red etc. This is a process of lightening the hair colour mainly for cosmetic purposes using bleaching agents. Bleaching can be done alone combined with a toner to get blond colour but for outstanding volume and toner bleach be used with colours. It is estimated that this barbering service should take 40 minutes working period, including applying colour/dye, waiting, washing & rinsing. All towels for drying must be provided.

LINES-UP & EDGES

This is a fine shape the edges of your hair into sharp lines. Normally this barbering service is performed on areas such as temples, partings, and significant hairlines. It is estimated that this barbering service should takes approximately 15-20 min. Make use of a trimmer clipper machine alone or shaving gel combined with barber straight razor.

HAIR STYLING

The art of arranging the hair in a particular style that is appropriately suited to the cut. There are various types of hair styling tools you need to style the hair like curling irons, hair straighteners, crimping irons, and hot rollers. These hair styling tools come in different sizes for example large barrel curling irons and wide straighteners are for long, thick hair and small barrel curling irons and thin straighteners are for short, fine hair. Clips and pins are also considered styling tools, as these tools come handy when creating updo styles or keeping top layers out of the way while curling or straightening under layers.

There are styling products which are used to keep styles in place and to maximize how long a hairstyle will hold up. Hairspray, gel, mousse, detangler and smoothing serum should all be in your toolbox as a barber/hairdresser.

2.2. BARBERING TOOLS FOR SERVICES

 CLIPPERS

 TRIMMER

 COMB

SHAVER

SCISSORS

STRAIGHT RAZOR

FACE BRASH

HAIR BRASH

 NECK BRASH

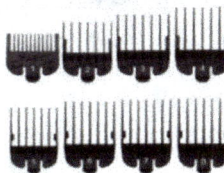 TWIST SPONGE

BARBER CAPE

GAURDS

2.3. BARBERING HAIR PRODUCTS

 **HOLD SPRAY**

 **APPLICATOR**

 **POMADE**

 **SHAVING GEL**

 **AIRBRUSH**

 **SHAMPOO**

 **HAIR FIBRE**

 **HAIR CONDITIONER**

2.4. BARBERING TOOLS MAINTENANCE PROCEDURES

It is very important how you take care of your barbering tools, whenever you fail to manage them well will results in loss due to damages, rust, malfunction and broken. The following picture shows you the products you need to have and use to properly maintain your barbering tools.

 Disinfecting glass bottle

 Blade spray

 Blade oil

Double edge blades

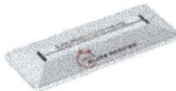 Blade Modifier

The following tips/or instructions will help you apply a proper way of maintaining your barbering tools so you can keep them clean, hygienic, and in good conditions to work for a long period without giving you problems.

Tip 1:
Make sure you always put blade oil on your clipper blades before use for smooth movement and free friction between the blades.

Tip 2:
Make use of a "1 min blade modifier" to keep your blades sharp and smooth to prevent friction between the blades and have smooth blade movement and speed.

Tip 3:
Keep your blades clean all the time by making use of a brush to remove any dirt or stuck hair on the blades.

Tip 4:
Avoid getting your clipper blades in contact with water to prevent the blades from rust, any liquid that meets your clipper blades will cause friction and rust so use a towel to wipe.

Tip 5:
Use disinfection spray on your clipper blades to prevent causing harm to your customer's skin.

Tip 6:
Keep the barber razors sharp all the time by using strops and whetstones to maintain these tools.

Tip 7:
Barbers are required by law to sterilize their tools between use to prevent the spread of germs. You need an autoclave and a UV

cabinet for sterilizing sheers and other supplies each time you use them.

Tip 8:
After work keep your blades, scissors, and razor inside the disinfection glass bottle to disinfect your sheers.

Tip 9:
Use the razor double edge blade to remove the dirt or the hair that got stacked in between the clipper blades and just pass the razor blade between the lower and upper blades of the hair clipper to push out the hair.

CHARPTER #3:

"BARBERING TOOLS & OPERATIONS"

3.1. HAIR CLIPPERS

A hair clipper it's a hand-held electronic machine designed to cut or remove hair. Normally it's a tool that is used in the barbering industry by barbers to cut human hair on the head area. A hair clipper is a specialized implement used to cut human head hair. They work on the same principle as scissors but are distinct from scissors themselves and razors. Similar but heavier-duty implements are used to shear sheep but are called headpieces or machine shears. The picture below shows an example of a hair clipper machine and its functions.

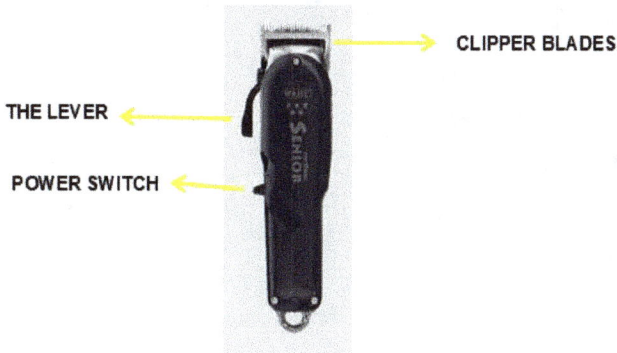

Firstly, every barber must know how to use a hair clipper as a barber, how it works, and its functions because how can one operate something they don't know how it works. It's easy to learn how a hair clipper works because it consists only of two main functions which are a "Lever" and a "Power switch" whereby a lever is used to adjust the blades and a power switch is used to turn the hair clipper power "ON" and "OFF". The pictures below provide you with a clear illustration of how to use both a "lever" and "power switch".

LEVER

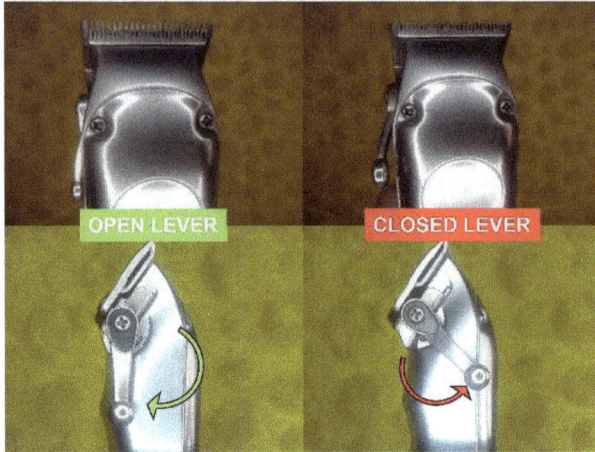

The following picture is the illustration of how to adjust the lever with your hand.

The following picture is the illustration of how to switch "on" and "off" the switch on the hair clipper machine.

POWER SWITCH

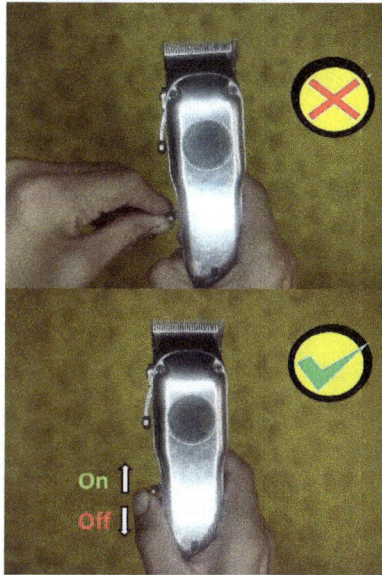

The picture below shows a proper way of holding the hair clipper machine in your hand when cutting hair with the top view illustration.

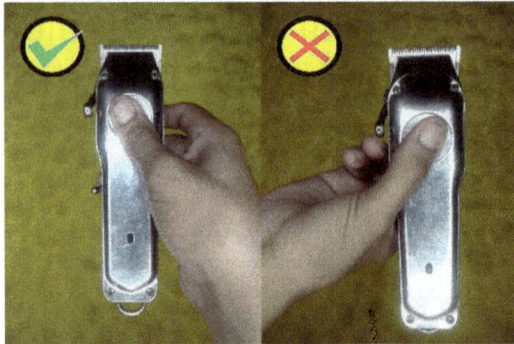

The picture below shows a proper way of holding the hair clipper machine in your hand when cutting hair with the side view illustration.

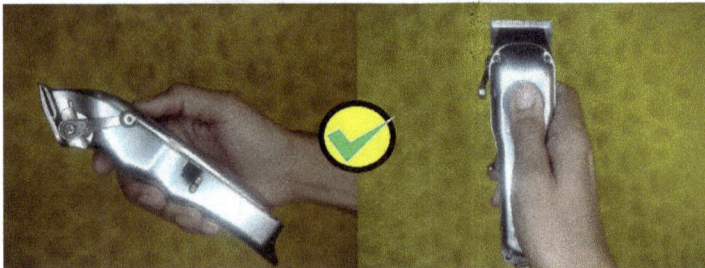

The pictures below give you a clear elastration of how a barber should properly hold a hair clipper machine when doing the line-up or hair line trimming.

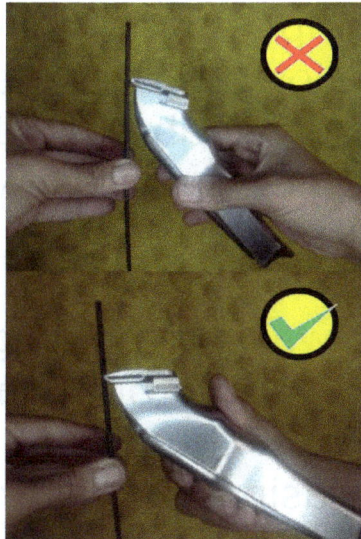

3.2. BARBER SCISSORS

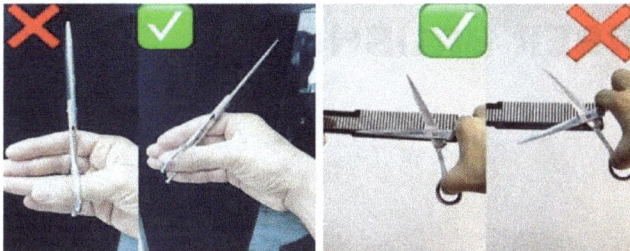

The pictures above give you a clear understanding and illustration of how a barber should properly hold or use a barber scissor. There are two ways of holding your barber scissors and comb in one hand. The first one is to take your thumb out of the handle and grip them using your little finger while allowing the blades to drop downwards. Your comb should be held in a way that it points upwards while one end sits on the palm.

There are two ways of holding your barber scissors and comb in one hand. The first one is to take your thumb out of the handle and grip them using your little finger while allowing the blades to drop downwards. Your comb should be held in a way that it points upwards while one end sits on the palm.

3.3 BARBER BRUSHES

Traditionally the barber brush is used to wipe away freshly cut hair on the nape of the neck and surrounding areas during and/or after a haircut. A traditional barbershop will typically have two types of brushes. One type of brush is used to dust hair from the customers clothing or neck after the barber is done. The other type is called the shaving brush. Barbers us a shaving brush to apply the foamy lather used to lessen irritation and provide a closer, more comfortable shave.

3.4. BARBER COMBS

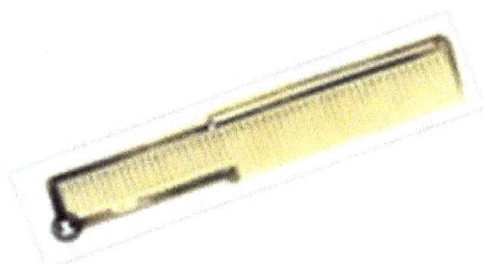

Combs are essential tools of the trade for barbers. Barbes uses combs for all obvious reasons, such as removing tangles, dividing hair into smaller sections for cutting, or making a clean part. However, they typically use a barber's comb which features teeth of graduated lengths and spacing to help them keep their cuts uniform as they trim each section.

A tapered barber comb can be used in the clipper over comb technique to blend and fade haircuts. The longer combs comb teeth can be used for shorter hair.

3.5. BARBER CAPE

A cape is a drape used to cover a customer while he is getting a haircut or other barbershop/salon services. It is used to keep hair off the customer.

3.6. BARBER RAZOR

A straight razor is a razor with a blade that can fold into its handle. They are also called open razors and cut-throat razors. The predecessors of the modern straight razors include bronze razors, with cutting edges and fixed handles, produced by craftsmen from Ancient Egypt during the New Kingdom. Solid gold and copper razors were also found in Ancient Egyptian tombs dating back to the 4th millennium BC.

An open blade on a handle and was used before the invention of the safety razor. Using one involves focusing to reduce the risk of cuts. Hydrate your face with hot water first and apply shaving soap with a brush. Hold the blade at an angle against your skin and move in short, controlled strokes.

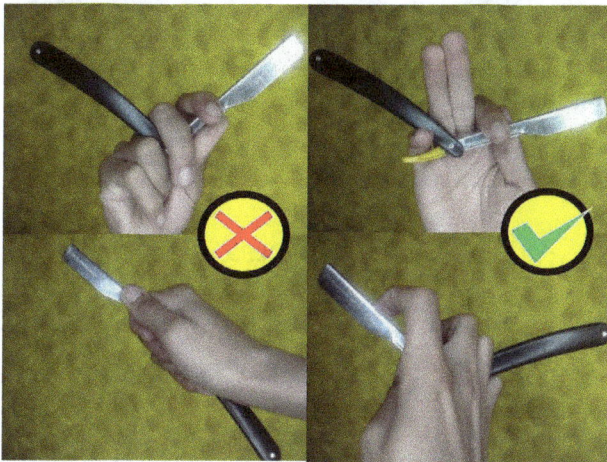

The picture above provides you with a clear illustration of how a barber should properly hold or use a barber razor. To hold the straight razor, put your first three fingers on the back of the blade and your pinkie on the tang, the upward curved metal bit at the end that looks like a little tail. Put your thumb on the side of the blade near the middle.

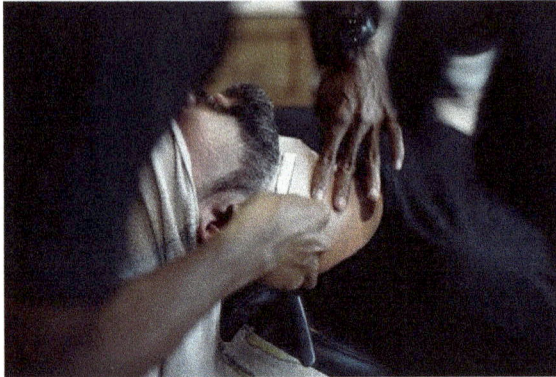

Shaving with a straight barber razor
Stretch the skin as taught as you can with your free hand (this is crucial when using cut-throats) and hold the blade against your skin at a 30- to a 35-degree angle. Anything steeper and you risk cutting yourself. It'll take practice to find just the right angle, but you'll be surprised at how quickly it becomes second nature. Do not fear coming over your head with your free hand to pull the skin as tight as it can go and use short, gentle strokes, letting the blade do the work. You are not quite

Edward Scissor hands remember. When shaving your neck lift your chin as high as it can go and pull the skin down from your neck. Pull your nose up to snag those tricky hairs under the nose.

CHARPTER #4:

"CLASSIC BARBER STRATEGY"

4.1. BARBERING INDUSTRY TERMINOLOGY

The barbering industry has a language, words and their meaning used as a form of communication in the industry. The industry requires that every barber, both beginner and professional must be able to interpret the language or terminology of the industry as it's a way of communicating in the industry. Understanding the industry language helps you to be communication effective and operate smoothly.

Have you ever walked in the barbershop and tried to articulate the hair style that you want to your barber? Or wondered how to explain the hair style you saw on your friend or that celebrity in magazine? Or watching tutorials on YouTube and could not understand any word spoken during the tutorial? We have all been there sweating and mumbling with no understanding of how to communicate our desires. Well, mumble no more, here is a list of barbershop terminology to equip yourself with.

HAIRCUT STYLES:

CLIPPER CUT
Same number of clipper guards all over. Same length hair all over the head.

FADE
Is when the hair on the sides of the head gradually gets shorter the farther down it goes. The hair eventually is reduced to nothing as it moves down towards the neck.

LOW FADE
Is when the hair disappears more than a few inches below the hairline.

HIGH FADE
In comparison to low fade, high fade is when the hair completely disappears within a few inches of the hairline.

MID FADE
Is when the fade ends somewhere in between a low fade and a high fade.

HIGH TOP FADE
Is a special kind of fade, it incorporates a fade on each side with long-but-flat hair on the top of the head.

BRUSH CUT
Brush is a process of cutting hair to a shorter length all around the head, leaving the hair light and short in length.

BALD CUT

Bald is completely removing the hair and leaving the head scalp with no hair, clean and smooth. In South Africa, we call it, "chieskop". Having a scalp wholly or partly lacking hair.

TAPPER FADE
A tapered haircut is short and surrounds the crown of the head. The haircut layers down from the crown towards the neckline. Each layer is tapered into the next, with a slightly shorter length than the previous level. The hair around the neckline is the shortest. There are two types of tapers, light and bald, and two placements of the taper, high and low.

BARBERING:

FLICK OUT MOTION
Flick out is a barber technique normally used for removing a visible guideline, this technique is done by touching the scalp with the blades from the beginning of the guideline and moving your hand wrist up and out movement.

GUIDELINE

A guideline's a line set by a barber around the crown of the head as a guide for the haircut process or strategy for fade or tapper. Section of hair, located at the perimeter of the interior of the cut that determines the length the hair will be cut to; usually, the first section that is cut to create a shape.

DRAPPING

The term used to describe the covering of the client's clothing with a cape for their protection.

HAIRCUT

The process of removing hair from the scalp of the head, which can be using a hair clipper, scissors, or shaver.

BARBER

A person who cuts men's hair and shaves or trims beards as an occupation.

FADE

Fade is a barber technique used to transition the haircut from bald to light to dark. There are two types of fades, light and bald, and two placements of the fade, high, medium, and low. The hair fades out.

TAPPER

Tapper is a barber technique whereby the haircut in which there is an even blend from very short at the hairline to longer lengths as you move up the head; to taper is to narrow progressively at one end.

LAYERS

Graduated effect achieved by cutting the hair with elevation or over direction; the hair is cut at higher elevations, usually, 90 degrees or above, which removes weight.

BLEND

Blend is a barber haircut technique of transitioning the hair from fine hair to thin hair and lastly to thick hair length. The hair blend in the length size of the hair whereby it gradually decreases from long hair length to a shorter hair length.

LEVEL
Unit of measurement to identify the lightness or darkness of a color.

FREEHAND
Razor position and stroke used in 6 of the 14 shaving areas: nos. 1, 3, 4, 8, 11, and 12.

FREE HAND CLIPPER CUTTING
Generally interpreted to mean that guards are not used in the cutting process.

FREE HAND SHEAR CUTTING
Cutting with shears without the use of fingers or a comb to control the hair.

NECK SHAVE
Shaving the areas behind the ears down the sides of the neck, and at the back neckline.

SHAVE

The shave is normally associated with a face area like cutting beards completely leaving the face skin smooth and clean.

BARBER TOOLS:

CLIPPER
Electric handheld haircutting tools with a single adjustable-blade or detachable-blade system.

TRIMMER
Small clippers, also known as outliners and edges, are used for detail, precision design, and fine finish work after a haircut or beard trim.

COMB
A strip of plastic, metal, or wood with a row of narrow teeth, used for untangling or arranging the hair.

BLADES
The cutting parts of the clippers, usually manufactured from high-quality carbon

steel and available in a variety of styles and sizes.

GUARDS
Plastic or hard rubber comb attachments that fit over clipper blades to minimize the amount of hair being cut with the clippers; or a metal shield applied over a haircutting razor for protection.

BARBER STRAIGHT RAZOR
Also known as open razor used to provide close shaves to customers without inflicting damage. They are also used to shave facial hair as well as trim the neckline.

SCISSOR
There are a variety of scissors, with different types serving different purposes. Straight-bladed scissors can be used to trim hair, beards, and mustaches. Smaller versions can be used to trim ear or nose hair. Special scissors with inset serrations can be used to thin or feather hair.

BRUSH

Is used to wipe away freshly cut hair on the nape of neck and surrounding areas during and/or after a haircut.

BARBER CAPE
A cape is a drape used to cover a customer while he/she is getting a haircut or other barbershop /salon services. Also used to keep hair off the customer.

HAIR:

HAIR GRAIN
Hair grain is the natural direction that the hair grows or facing.

SCALP
The skin covers the head, excluding the face.

HAIR CONDITIONER
Products are designed to moisturize the hair or restore some of the hair's oils or proteins.

HAIR COLOURING/DYE

An industry-coined term referring to artificial hair coloring products and services; the addition of color on or into the hair shaft.

HAIR STYLING
The art of arranging the hair in a particular style that is appropriately suited to the cut.

HAIR SERVICE PRODUCTS:

SHAMPOO
Removes dirt, oil, perspiration, and skin debris from the hair and scalp.

SHAMPOOS
Hair and scalp cleansing products

CONDITIONER
Chemical agents are used to deposit protein or moisturizers in the hair.

CONDITIONING SHAMPOOS
Also known as moisturizing shampoos, are mild cream shampoos that contain moisturizing agents (humectants) designed

either to "lock-in" the moisturizing properties of the product or to draw moisture into the hair.

4.2. THE ART OF FADE

The art of fading is the beauty of fade or the uniqueness of fade which can be described as a transition that starts from bald, to light, and dark. That transition is the art that makes fade to be awesome. Now the artwork of fade comes with a strategy and the strategy consist of different levels of guideline all around the crown of the head whereby they are separated by an inch or half an inch from each other, and this is the strategy it takes to produce the art of fade. The pictures below show you the process from the artwork to the result of the faded haircut. We call this artwork or strategy "classic barber strategy" which can be applied to have a quality fade haircut, clean and smooth.

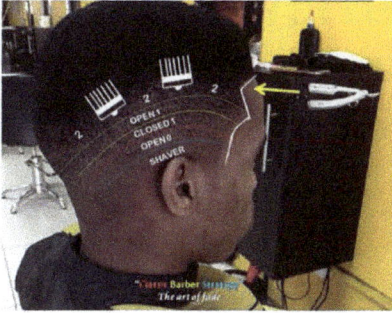

CLASSIC BARBER STRATEGY

FADE HAIRCUT

The picture above is a clear example of a process of a fade haircut from the strategy to results, using "classic barber strategy". For a barber to be able to perform the kind of fade haircut on the above picture he/she must learn our strategy. Below we have provided you with step-by-step guide on how you can apply the strategy and produce the kind of fade that is unique, clean, and smooth. Once you have learned the strategy you will be able to apply the strategy for any fade haircut and get reliable 100% results and quality fade haircut just by simply following the same step-by-step guide of "classic barber strategy" provided below.

4.3. CLASSIC BARBER STRATEGY STEP-BY-STEP

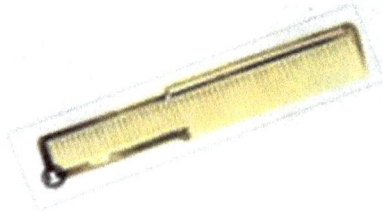

#STEP 1

Take your hair comb and start combing the customer's hair with the grain (in the direction of the hair growth) from the top of the crown on the head down to the Earline and down to the neckline making sure the hair is stretch and flexible. The customer's hair must be dry, not wet.

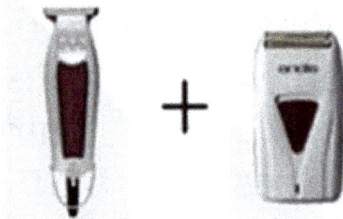

#STEP 2

Take your trimmer and face it down with the blades touching the scalp an inch above the Earline and start your first bald guideline moving all around the crown of the head on the sides and back. As you set your bald guideline at the back of the head make sure it's at least 3 inches above the neckline. After your bald guideline now cut the hair below the guideline to bald using your trimmer and final touch using your shaver for a smooth and clean bald.

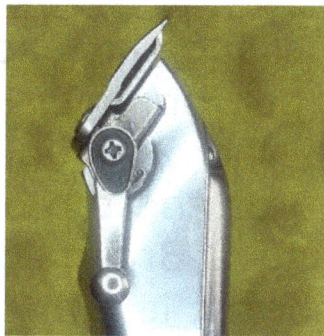

#STEP 3

Take your hair clipper and adjust your lever to open with no guard on your blades. Start from your bald line moving an inch up to form a second guideline above the first guideline. The second guideline will be light hair thin in length. As you cut against the grain keep brushing the hair with the grain.

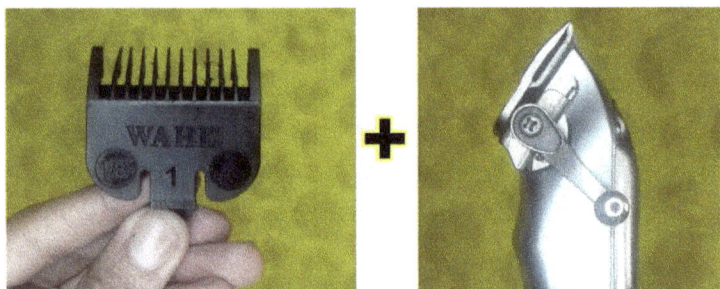

#STEP 4
Take your hair clipper and adjust the lever to closed and put on your no #1 guard. Beginning from the 2nd guideline moving up an inch towards the top of the crown of the head forming a 3rd guideline that will give you the shortest length of hair.

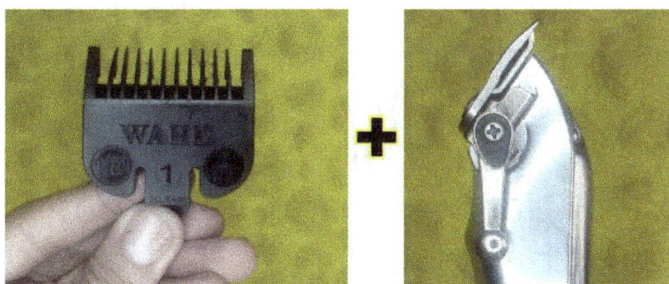

#STEP 5

Take your hair clipper and adjust your lever to full open and put on your no #1 guard. Beginning from the 3rd top guideline moving up an inch towards the top crown of the head forming the 4th guideline which will give you shorter dark hair in length.

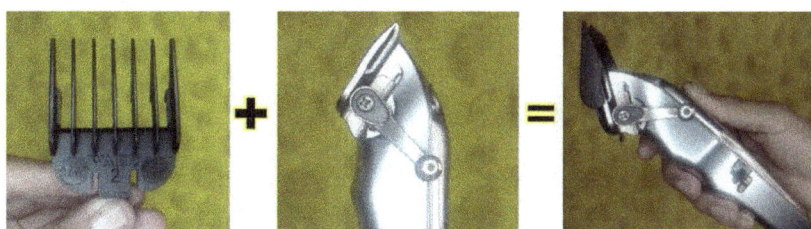

#STEP 6

Take your hair clipper with the lever adjusted to close and put on your no #2 guard. Beginning from the top end of the 4th guideline moving up and half an inch towards the crown of the head with a flick out the motion (up and out motion) and form the 5th guideline. This last guideline with combine with the hair on top of the crown of the head and will give you dark short length hair.

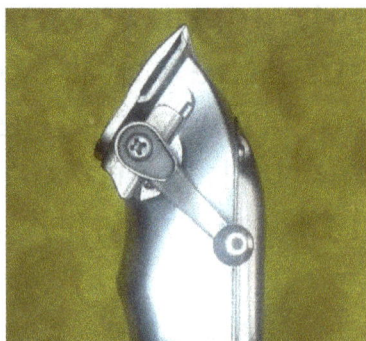

#STEP 7
Now that your guidelines are in place, different layers gradually increase up to the top of the crown of the head. Take your hair clipper with your lever adjusted to a closed position with no guard. Start to flick out the

1st bald guideline half an inch within the guideline level without touch the top end of the guideline. This will remove the visible low guideline to form a transition.

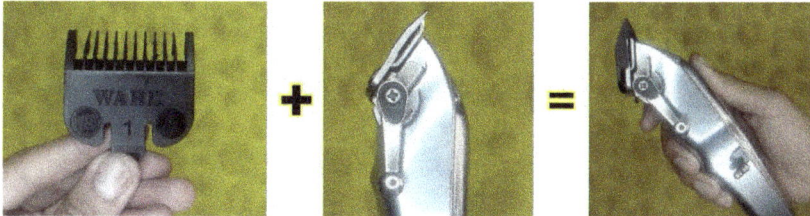

#STEP 8

Now that you cleared the lower bald guideline from the 1st guideline. Take your hair clipper and put on your no #1 guard. Move half an inch in each guideline level with a flick-out motion using the corners of your clipper blades to clear all low visible guidelines. Each guideline is guided by the previous one as you move up. This will give you a clear and smooth transition of fade.

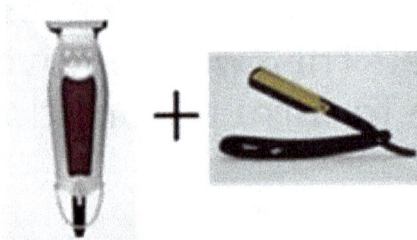

#STEP 9

Now that you are done with the fade process move to the line-up or trimming. Take your trimmer facing down and set your guideline at the beginning of the hairline on the four heads. Move from the centre to left and centre to right side toward each corner of the four head making sure the line-up is balanced and straight. Now take your barber straight razor for a clean and smooth line-up.

#STEP 10

The last step is to take your comb and comb the entire hair on the top of the crown of the head making sure it's stretched and flexible then take your hair clipper with the lever adjusted to a closed position without a guard. Move on the surface on the top hair and on the side around the crown of the head to clear out all unbalanced hair ends. You will have a clean final bald low fade haircut.

CHARPTER #5:

"BARBER'S PERSONAL DEVELOPMENT"

5.1. CHARACTER

Character is one of the main factors that play a huge role in the barbershop business and the relationship between your business and customers. Character it's an attitude or in simple term is a personality. Character is the product of your believe or philosophy(mindset). Your barbershop will take on your personality as the owner, your employees will behave like you. Character is more often displayed and seen by how you treat other people. People feed from our character, it's either they are hungry for you or fed up with you. To be a professional barber you must have a good character. Below we have provided you with a list of factors that contribute good character:

BE HUMBLE

Humbleness attracts favour, but pride and ego send your customers away from you. Be humble and always willing to listen to your customers about what they want and how they want it so you can provide the service exactly how the customer requested. When you are humble it's easy to obey instructions even when you think you know better, or you are the best. Customers are very sensitive so don't assume but rather suggest with humility what may best work for your customer. Your humbleness will attract customers and your Pride will chase them away.

VALUE AND RESPECT CUSTOMERS

How you treat your customers determines if your relationship with them will go for a long run or be cut off in a short period. A business dealing with people requires a person that can tolerate others as you will be dealing with different characters and personalities. It's advisable to always keep a good attitude even when your customer is wrong. Behaviour is very important it either feeds your customers or they get fed up with you as a barber. Good qualities such as humbleness, self-control, kindness, humility, respect, patience, are very priceless but being rude, disrespectful, and proud to your customers it's a bad character for the barbershop business.

BE PEOPLE ORIENTATED
Being a barber requires you to be a people person, as you will be dealing with people on daily basis in your business environment. You must love people and understand people's differences as you will meet different kinds of people, characters, and personalities. Learn how to communicate with your customers and

building relationships. Listen to your customers and ask them questions. Give them a sense of belonging. Be open for discussion. Never argue with your customers.

HAVE LOVE

Having love for people is when you put other people's needs first before yours. It's important to understand that customers are, the boss to the barber because they are the ones that pay the barber. Care about customers happiness and satisfaction. A happy and satisfied customer is a returning customer. You can only lose customers by being selfish and not considerate to make them happy by giving them your best service.

COMMUNICATE WITH YOUR CUSTOMERS

As a professional barber, you should be able to build a relationship with your customers. Without communication, any relationship cannot be established. Interacting with your customers. It's important, to know that you don't just receive a customer on your barber chair and perform a haircut service and let the customer go without communication. Sometimes it's advisable to know your customers by name as it creates a sense of recognition. Ask your customers questions like how was your day? Where are you from? Which language do you speak etc? Listen to your customers on how they want the haircut service to be done or how they prefer it to be done, don't just assume. Giving a customer what they want and the way they want it, will grow your business, and keep them coming back next time.

BE APPROACHABLE
Always keep a smile on your face. People are attracted to a happy person; the energy or atmosphere of a happy person is fruitful for other people to find themselves in. Your customers must always feel free to talk to you or ask you questions. A barber must always build a relationship with his customers.

MANAGE YOUR EMOTIONS

Have a way of controlling yourself or your emotions on bad days. when you are treated with disrespect in the work environment or when you are upset about bad news or having a bad day. A customer service business deals with different kinds of people and personalities so you must know how to deal with different people in different situations. Put your emotions in control all the time because they determine your performance. Never be found in an argument or fight with your customers. Be the master of your emotions, put them under your control.

5.2. BARBERING SKILL

Make sure you deliver experience and quality. Today it seems like everyone can cut hair, and if you are coming into the industry as a barber that can only cut hair then the world already is full of barbers who can cut hair but few who can deliver quality and satisfaction to customers. Make haircutting your gift, refine it and improve it by consistently practicing, and gaining knowledge with the trends and issues surrounding the industry and be a solution. Solve a problem and that's what will set you apart from all the other barbers.

Master your craft and be good at it that when people think about it, your name comes in their minds. Hone your skill and have a solid strategy for a haircut. The more you work on improving the skill will upgrade your value to a professional or specialist level in the barbering industry. Consistently give quality results and continually practice your strategy to master it.

5.3. CUSTOMER SERVICE

Customer service is the reason for the value of your product or service, the best customer service gets the best customer response. Barbers must maintain providing customers with the consistent quality of haircuts. Your service has your name on it meaning a bad service is bad for the name of the business. In the barbering industry, customer service is one of the main factors that play a huge role in the growth of the barbershop business, at barber classic cuts, our customers are our boss because they bring money into the business. The classic barber's goal is to keep his customers happy all the time, the happiness of his/her customers must be a priority. Below we have provided you with a list of factors that contribute to a successful barbering customer service.

BE PRESENT ALL THE TIME AT THE SHOP

The barbershop business cannot operate outside or without a barber inside the barbershop because when people come to the barbershop is to see the barber and to get their hair fixed by the barber. A classic barber is the one who you will forever find in the barbershop whenever you need him, and this requires patience for a barber to stay in the barbershop even when customers are not there but because the shop without a barber cannot be a barbershop then a barber should always stay in the barbershop. Customers must always find the barber waiting in the barbershop to serve them not the other way around whereby the customer is waiting for the barber who is not inside the barbershop.

TIME MANAGEMENT

Always find the quickest way to deliver a haircut service in a short waiting period with the least amount of effort. Most customers hate waiting too long before they can get their service. In general waiting period for a haircut should take about 20-30 minutes per customer. A customer in the queue is expected to wait at least a maximum of 1 hour before they can get a haircut service. People hate waiting too long before they can get a service and wait again too long before the barber can finish the service. Create a system that can give customers the best quality service in the less waiting period using the least amount of effort that's a great time management goal for the business.

LOVE WHAT YOU DO(WORK)

Your focus determines where your energy will go. You can know what you love based on where your focus is. You lose energy fast doing things you don't love because automatically your focus is somewhere else. If you love what you do, then the work easy to do without getting tired. Everything you do without love becomes a burden. For good results, you must love what you do because where you put your focus you can't make mistakes. A classic barber must be service driven.

BE CONSISTENT

Consistency creates reliability. Being consistent in the quality of your services and your working hours is what grows the business. The consistent quality barbering service makes customers know when they come to your barbershop what to expect and it protects the name or brand of the business. Customers are attracted to the disciplined business because they want a place they can rely on and get what they expect from the place without being disappointed. Maintain reproduction of good quality results at all costs to give your brand a name and recognition in the community.

SOLVE YOUR CUSTOMERS PROBLEMS
In most cases, a barber comes across different situations and people of different hairlines. Some customers come from another barbershop where they were messed up and you need to be able to give a solution for every problem you come across because people are paid for the problems they solve. You are paid for the problems you are solving in your area of influence of work.

PROVIDE QUALITY SERVICES
The quality of a product or service determines its value. In the barbering

industry, your work speaks for you. The quality of service you provide and the consistency in working hours are what give the clients the reliability to know when they come to your barbershop what to expect. Results are always a testimony.

5.4. PRESENTATION

Presentation is the face/image of the company; people will always judge a book by its cover. So how you present yourself in business will determine what kind of clients or customers you attract to your business as its part of the marketing tools. A classic barber must look presentable and highly present the brand effectively to pull the right crowd. Presentation is everything when it comes to the growth and expansion of the business. Presentation is the face of the company as it is the display of the business. The identity of the business it's in its presentation. The quality of the display determines how people will value it. The company's image predicts what it stands for, and what to expect. They say, "The first impression lasts forever." this statement suggest that customers have different personalities, taste, values, and preferences. Based on the company's presentation it will determine if it loses or attracts customers. Below we have provided you with a list of factors that contribute to the successful presentation as a classic barber.

DEVELOP A DRESS CODE POLICY

A dress code is part of the company policy so it must comply or compliment the company's logo, colours, and concept. There are different kinds of dress codes in the work environment like formal, casual, and PPE (personal protective equipment) depending on the nature of the work environment. The company uniform makes the company professional and trustworthy to customers.

BE CLEAN

A barber must always wear clean clothes and smell good. Making sure the workstation is clean all the time. The tools and equipment used by the barbers must always be cleaned properly and maintained with care. Cleanness is next to Love, your love for something is seen by how you treat or take care of it. Love yourself as a barber and look clean all the time because clients will treat you how you treat yourself.

5.5. BARBER WORKSTATION

The barber workstation is his place of performance, work, and interaction with the customers. A classic barber station is a station that is well organized and clean all the time. Whereby tools and equipment are placed in their right place and space is available for both the barber and the customer. Barber station is the barber's work environment, and that environment must be conducive for barbering. The Barber station consists of a barber chair, mirror, wall cupboard, and tools and equipment.

BE ORGANIZED

Put your tools and products in order, keep your barber station clean and well structured. Know where you put things and where or how you can get them. Don't be a chaotic barber who puts things everywhere and struggles to find them due to forgetting where he/she placed them. It saves time to be organized because you don't have to waste time looking for something.

CHARPTER #6:

"SETTING-UP A BARBERSHOP BUSINESS"

6.1. BARBERSHOP BUSINESS PLAN

Do not make assumptions that your business will work some day without making any analysis or projections. You must think through business modelling or competition and how you will deal with it. "If you fail to plan, you are planning to fail!". Business planning is not a destination but a journey, in simple terms I mean we don't go to it, but we grow through it. Business planning it's a sign of your faith in something and it's a lifelong commitment.

BUSINESS PLAN

Write down your vision on a paper and be honest with yourself based on where you are currently and where you want to get and how you going to get there. A business plan creates a roadmap for your business. Helping you navigate your business when you hit rough patches in your shop. It helps you in times of expansion and when you need to raise funds from investors. It helps you to keep your business on course and be able to adjust based on your plan. It can also help you in terms of your business expansion. Develop a business plan that is details operating costs, start-up costs, advertising costs, staff requirements, anticipated clientele, and how you intend to compete. Create analysis for the target market, industry, customer, and competitors.

6.2. BARBERSHOP BUSINESS REQUIREMENTS

INDUSTRY REQUIREMENTS:

There are different requirements and expectations for being a barber or running a barbershop business for different countries. In America for one to start a barbershop he/she must obtain a barbershop permit from your state cosmetology board or licensing department and pay required fees depending on what kind of barbershop business you want to run.

GOVERNMENT REQUIREMENTS

Get your business registered and file paperwork for a corporate, sole proprietorship, private, Pty, Ltd, LLC. For South African citizens you must get your business name registered with CIPC, open a business bank account, and make sure you comply with SARS and file taxes for your business. Make sure your business working hours for your employees comply with the department of labour.

INSURANCE REQUIREMENTS

Get an insurance policy for your business to cover it in times of uncertainty of circumstances or unexpected challenges in your business.

LEGAL REQUIREMENTS
Hire an attorney to review the details of the lease agreement with the landlord such as the landlord's responsibility with repairs, expansion potential, early lease termination clause, and what happens if an adjacent business moves out.

SECURITY REQUIREMENTS
Install alarm system and cameras for security purposes and safety of the business.

6.3. BUSINESS FUNDING

There are many ways to raise funds for your business. You can start a business without cash, all you need to start a business is you. Let me give you ways in which you can raise funds for your business:

WORK

Most independent barbershop owners today began in the business by working for someone else's shop and felt they could succeed on their own. Start working for an already established salon or barbershop business and start saving money from your salary to open your own business.

CLIENTS

Based on the skill you have; you can offer it as a service to your customers that they might pay you for your skill then from the money they pay you then you can start saving for opening your barbershop business.

INVESTORS

Approach investors with your business plan with financial projections which states, how much you need and what you need it for, then how much you will make in your business and how you plan to pay them back)

BANKS OR FINANCIAL INSTITUTIONS

Get a loan for your business of which I normally don't recommend for starter businesses because normally banks don't offer money to people who need it but to those who have a track record of doing business. Get a loan from the bank only for expanding your business not for starting.

FAMILY AND FRIENDS

Ask for financial assistance from those you are related with, which they will give you money based on their sympathy. It's important to pay back your relatives when they have borrowed you, their money.

SMALL BUSINESS PARTNERSHIP

Partner your business with already established manufacturing companies which produce products related to barbering. You can become their supplier, distributor, or a reseller of their products. You can get the products at a stock price and sell at your desired price and from the profit you make then you can save to start your own business.

6.4. SETTING-UP A BARBERSHOP BUSINESS

You cannot run a successful barbershop business with only the skill of cutting hair, you need more than that to manage a business. Skills you need are mostly non-barbering such as accounting, bookkeeping, negations with the landlord, marketing, and sales skill. Things to note down as you start your own barbershop business. Your barbershop will take on your personality. Running your barbershop offers financial stability. You will have freedom and control over your finances. Small businesses come with benefits and advantages. They provide tax breaks, partnerships with other companies and sell their products and make some money and freedom to take control of your destiny.

BARBERSHOP EQUIPMENT SHEET

The following list below will help you know the things you will need to start a barbershop business.

BARBERSHOP EQUIPMENT SHEET FROM BCC BARBERSHOP

Barbershop equipment check list:

BARBERSHOP FECILITIES	BARBERSHOP TOOLS	BARBERSHOP HAIR PRODUCTS
RECEPTION	**BARBER TOOLS**	**BARBER STATION HAIR PRODUCTS**
○ Reception desk	○ Wahl clipper – detailer	○ Hair fibre
○ Reception chair	trimmer	○ Hold spray.
○ Retail display cupboard	○ Wahl clipper – 5-star magic	○ Pomade
○ Telephone	○ Wahl shaver – 5-star	○ Shaving gel
○ Barbershop management software	○ Shaving barber razor	○ After shave cream
○ Wi-fi router	○ Scissors	
○ Appointment booking/scheduling software	○ Comb set	**SHAMPOO STATION HAIR PRODUCTS**
	○ Razor blades	○ Hair conditioner
	○ Clipper guards	○ Shampoo
○ PC	○ Neck collar paper	○ Hair spray
○ Cash register	○ Neck brush	○ Colours/Dye (black)
	○ Beard hand brush	○ Colours/Dye (blonde/bleach)
CUSTOMER WAITING AREA	○ Mirror – double grip	○ Colours/Dye (red, green, blue, & purple)
○ Waiting area chairs		○ Colours/Dye (white)
○ Wall mounted TV set	**MAINTENANCE**	
○ Bar Table	○ Blade modifier	
○ Magazine/newspaper rack	○ Disinfections jar	
○ Pool game table	○ Wahl oil – clipper oil	
○ Fridge	○ Blade disposable container	
	○ Cool care – Andis blade spray	
BARBER STATIONS	○ Disinfection spray	
○ Wall mounted mirrors		
○ Wall mounted cupboards	**SHAMPOO STATION TOOLS**	
○ Barber cape	○ Aprons	
○ Wall mounted clipper holder	○ Colour mixer	
○ Lighting (Ring lights)	○ Spray bottles	
	○ Tint bowl	
SHAMPOO STATIONS	○ Tint brush	
○ Shampoo unit (backwash & chair)	○ Towels	
○ Wall mounted cupboards	○ Hair dryer	
○ Dryer stands and chair.		
○ Washing machine (for towels)		
○ Carts & Trolleys		

BARBERSHOP FURNITURE & EQUIPMENTS

The barbershop has different facilities like reception, shampoo station, barber station, customer waiting area, and retail products display area.

Reception tables

Reception chairs

Shampoo chairs

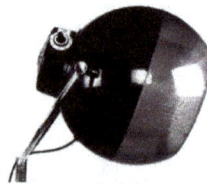
Stand Dryer

Barber chairs

Waiting chairs

Wall mirrors

Wall cupboard

PRODUCTS AND SERVICES
Determine what services and products you are going to offer based on the previous employers or local competition and create a competitive price list based on your local competition. Create a competitive pricing list to determine what kind of profit you can expect to make and how much you can afford to spend on rent and other business expenses. Develop your business S.W.O.P to determine what makes you different from the rest of your local competitors.

BUSINESS CONCEPT
Establish the business theme of how you want your business to look and what kind of people are your target market. Creating an environment that is suitable and feels like home for your target market. This is where your vision of the business is displayed. Concepts are different like a barbershop that is mixed with a salon as they coexist well with one another, or a male salon, sports theme, car lovers' theme, workout theme, etc.

BUSINESS MODELING

This is a process of how you are going to distribute your product until it reaches your consumer. Unlike business plan, business modelling analysis the past and what makes the existing business to stand but business plan gives projections of the future. Business modelling will help you identify what kind of business you should start or work for you. Determine what kind of barbershop you want to start. There are many ways to start a barbershop business such as:

- **BUYING EXISTING BUSINESS**
  buying an existing barbershop whereby the owner wants to sell their shop, it comes with the equipment and employees. or
- **FRANCHISE MODEL**
  Buying a brand barbershop business, and pay royalties which comes with name reputation and ack record, consistent quality product or
- **START-UP MODEL**

Start your business from the scratch and have your own barbershop.

- **PARTNERSHIP MODEL**
  Get into partnership with clipper brands companies such as Whal, Andis, BaByliss etc. to resell their product in your barbershop or become a supplier. Adding retail barbering products in your business gives your business the advantage of generating extra income outside barbering services.

6.5. LOCATION

Choosing a location for your business can either make or break your business. When choosing a location make sure you choose a place that is already zoned for barbering and is near other supporting businesses that your clientele frequents like shopping centres, this will significantly reduce your workload and illuminate the need for a building permit or zoning approval. There are important things to look out for when you scout out for a potential location for your business that can help your business grow. Look for a place that is visible in the streets, that has enough packing to accommodate the growth that has walking traffic. Generally, your rent should not exceed 10% of your projected gross revenue.

BUSINESS ENVIRONMENT

Determine your floor plan and structure of working operation. Keep the workplace always clean, hygienic, and smelling good all the time. Let the business set up comply with the barbershop concept. Display colours that complement the company logo and employee uniform. Let the business structure be well organized and easy to interpret by your customers for waiting area, reception, barber station, shampoo station, etc.

6.6. EMPLOYMENT

Team execution is one of the most important factors in the success of the business. Teamwork makes a dream come true. If you don't understand people, you stand no chance running a successful business. Business is a democracy, done by people, for the people, and through people. Don't build a business but build people and those people will build your business. The rich work smart and the poor work hard, this simply mean the poor work hard with their hands and the rich work hard using other people's hands to do what they cannot do for themselves. Here are some of key principles of building your team:

- **ROLE MODEL YOUR TEAM**
  You cannot take people where you have never been, firstly take a journey to a place and invite them over. Don't tell them what to do but show them what to do by Leading them by examples, because they can only do what you do. Your business will take on your personality. Model the language you want your team to use. Treat your team like how you want them to treat your best client. Model the behaviour you want them to use. Encourage your team to avoid gossip.

- **PROTECT YOUR TEAM EMOTIONALLY**

  Correct them in private and don't tear them in public. Let them know that you want to protect them emotionally. Your team has the same desires and needs just like you, to have a house, a car, and live so make sure you care about their needs. When they see that you care, they will care for your business. They care how much you care not how much you have. Communicate your vision consistently to them, when there's faith in the future, there's power in the present. Timid employees are the reflection of an intimidating boss, but confident employees are the reflection of a boss who consistently assures them over and over again. You don't produce who you want but who you are. You produce after your kind or type.

- **UNDERSTAND YOUR TEAM**

  People are not the same, they have different temper and personalities. They are going through different seasons in their lives. They work at different speed. Don't compare your team not even customers. Don't say to them, "if you were there! things would have been done better!", they are not you, and we are all different.

- **CONNECT WITH YOUR TEAM**
Create time to get to know them. Go out with them once a time and build a human environment, attend their events, speak to them, ask how they feel and know what they are going through. Be concern about them.

- **COMMUNICATE WITH YOUR TEAM**
Don't leave your team guessing or making assumptions about things but rather communicate with them. Make them see things how you see them. Don't expect them to know what you didn't communicate to them.

- **LISTEN TO YOUR TEAM**
Don't listen to your team with the attitude of responding but listen as if you will make presentation from what was spoken. You learn a lot from just listening, listen to hear not only what is

being said but also what was not said. When you are listening then you get to know what they know and what they don't know.

- **EMPATHISE WITH YOUR TEAM**
Empathy is not sympathy therefore don't feel for them but feel with them, try to be in their shoes. Acknowledge their emotions/feelings even if you disagree with them. Refuse to be judgemental or to belittle their feelings. Understand that feelings are not either positive or negative, but they are just feelings. Don't fight over feelings. Learn to respond not to react, don't lose your cool and don't lose your composure. No one is perfect.

- **SEE THE GOOD IN YOUR TEAM**
Motivate and encourage your team with good words. What we praise is likely to flourish than what we condemn. In every person you will get what you are looking for either positive or negative, good, or bad. Dig for the gold and take out the best in your team.

- **BELIEVE IN YOUR TEAM**
  Show your team that you trust them, and they will go extra mile to prove their trustworthy to you but show them you don't trust them then they will prove you right.

HIRING

Firstly, when it comes to hiring, I don't recommend that you start looking from people you know like families, friends, or relatives. Hiring beginner barbers or cosmetology students which are barbers in training at barbering schools can require you to train them how you want then to cut at your shop. Hire well-groomed barbers or licensed barbers. Finding skilled barbers can be very difficult. If hiring contractors, ensure that they have liability insurance coverage.

BUSINESS SYSTEM

Develop the barbershop business system. A business system will help you have employees and run your business successfully. Business system is when the business can function outside the owner's presence. Products can make you money, but a business system can make you a fortune. A great business system attracts people who are smarter and more talented than the owner because they feel secured in a business with a system. Business system should have a clear stuffing, operational, cashflow, communication, system. The business system should be scalable, if it works in this place then it can work at any place. Decide on how you intend to run your business from customers to employees. The Working hours and operational workflow of the business. The system governs the structure of the company from the manager to the supervisor, to the employees, and lastly to the customers. The business system covers all the operations of the business. Develop a code of conduct in the business for employees which will state the employee requirements and duties. Develop a dress code policy for your employees.

6.7. COMPETITION

We have failed in the concept of mastery because we want to copy what others are doing. Every industry has competition more especially when you are making money in your area of business, that's where everyone will come running and start a business in that area. People want to do what you are doing if they see the results you produce, then they want to copy and do what you are doing. That's the reason we have competition in the area of businesses. When it comes to competition you need to study those that are leading businesses in the industry you want to get into because they are a visible sign of success. We don't study them to copy them but to emulate their success and embed your vision in it with taste of creativity, innovativeness, and genuine business dealings. This is what sets you apart from the rest and ask yourself, "what problem are you solving in the industry?". You become valuable when what you do is rare and when you have mastered your craft in your work. One of the things that can make you stand out is when you can offer the best quality service in less time than normal and with the least amount of effort. You must be a specialist in your field and master your work to a point that you cannot be replaced. Do what you do so well that when people think about it, your picture and your name come into their minds. When you stand out you become a recommendation.

6.8. MARKETING STRATEGY

Develop a plan on how you intend to reach your target market. The marketing strategy depends entirely on the market you intend to target. Firstly, study the demographics and local market. Offer discounts to your existing clientele for a customer referral. Host a grand opening, submit a press release, and get your barbershop listed in local directories. Start a website for your shop. Do a window advertising on your barbershop for the walking traffic.

CHARPTER #7:

"BARBERING PRODUCTS INVENTORY"

7.1. PRODUCTS INVENTORY

Product inventory is a result of an idea. Business ideas are more powerful than any source of capital. Ideas attract investors and when you have a sound idea, nobody cares about your gender, age, race because ideas rule the world. The real test of an idea is its ability to solve a real human problem. An idea that does not solve a human problem will face existence challenges. The problem you avoid solving in your neighborhood/city/nation/place of work can be an idea that is sustainable. Money will come and go but human problems will persist. The more the stubborn persistence negging human problem, the greater business idea. Problems are an opportunity to come up with ideas.

There are two ways to go about doing product inventory, which is the route of "Private label", which is a process in which you take an existing product and change its brand name to your brand name and the other way of product inventory is to create a product from the scratch which is a process I recommend as it will give you copyrights of your product and make your product different from the rest. The first step in product inventory you should come up with an idea for your product. The motivation should be to solve a problem and not to make money, it should be a product you are passionate about. Find a problem and create a product that will solve that problem. Ask yourself what it is that you wish existed and doesn't exist and how you can make it a better product. You want to create something that is new, unique, and better. That can be as simple as taking something that exists and making it better.

7.2. PRODUCT CREATION

Determine what products you want to sell, and if that product will close the gap in the market or provide a solution to the market need. You can make a product from a can existing product and simply make it better. You can create your own product from scratch. After identifying the product, you want to sell then get a logo which will be a label for the product or a trademark. In the product creation stage, there will be many fees involved.

The manufacturing company will charge you a fee to digitalize your brand or logo which is known as the artwork fee. Then the other fee will be for the printing of your brand design on the product container. Then the other fee will be for the kind of container your product should be made from, which is the material. Then lastly, they will charge you a fee for packaging material and bar code. During the creation process the designer will be showing you mockup designs to confirm the look of how you want the product to look like. Then the product should move from digital to physical product once you have approved everything.

7.3. FINDING A MANUFACTURING COMPANY

There's a website called "Alibaba" or "Ali-express", where you can find a different kinds of manufacturing companies which manufacture different products for all industries. Some of this manufacturing companies are based China, and they have affordable quotes. Not all companies listed in the platform are reliable and trustworthy so you will need to do a background check and investigation on the company you are interested to work with. Make sure you know all the details of the manufacturing company you choose to work with like the company name, what products they produce, where are they located, company certificates, years in business, business type: manufacturing or trading, product certificate, reviews, trade assurance and verification status from the platform.

Most of the time you will find a supplier company which are simply the middleman between you as the client and the manufacturing company. They are also known as trading companies which have a track record with the manufacturing company and have built a good working relationship which gives them the advantage to get low prices and benefits.

7.4. NEGOTIATIONS

You need to be able to negotiate the prices with your manufacturing company or supplier at the level of your affordability and strength. Give them reasons why you negotiate the price that meets your strength keeping in mind you will pay for other cost like shipping, duties and taxes and you don't know how the product will turn out in the market. Manufacturing companies make money from you as their client, and you make money from selling to the market, so basically you both need each other. Promise them a long working relationship, and to make large orders on your second order once you have started operating and finding out how the first order products turn out in the market. Establish a good working relationship with these manufacturing companies and let them become your supplier.

7.5. PRODUCTS PACKAGING

Product packaging is very important if you wish to distribute your product and sell it in big stores. The manufacturing company have fees involved with packaging which are based on the material type that will be used for your packaging, fees for the cover design of the box, fees for the barcode for your product, for some manufacturing companies the product barcode can be provided free. Each product is required to have its own unique bar code which will be printed on the product packaging. This bar code helps to identify the product.

7.6. PRODUCT ORDER

SAMPLE ORDER
Before you make your large order request a sample order to test the quality of the product and verify the product. When you are satisfied with the sample product then you can go ahead with making a large order, but all manufacturing companies have what we call "MOQ".

MOQ (MINIMUM ORDER QUANTITY)
Every manufacturing company has a standard minimum order quantity for each product you want to customize/brand. This helps the manufacturing company not to set up the machines and run the production process in a loss because there are expenses or costs for manufacturing

companies to set up their machines which include patrol, electricity etc. Therefore, for them to make a profit and not work on a loss, a MOQ is required.

7.7. PRODUCT SHIPPING

Shipping is a way to get your products from the manufacture to where you are, depending on your location fess may differ which are relied on how far you are. Shipping can be locally, provincially, or internationally. Shipping is the imports and exports duties. For international shipping from USA or UK, you can make use of third parties courier companies such as, "MyUS" which is a forwarding agent that can ship all around the world and provide you with an address in US and United Kingdom. The address can be used for receiving products or storage. Moreover, we have other reliable courier companies such as DHL, and FedEx which provide shipping services worldwide. If you are based in South Africa there are hand to hand courier companies or local courier companies like Aramex, you can rely on for sending your customers products locally. There are different kinds of shipping methods you can choose from depending on how long or quick you want your products delivered to you such as cargo, ship, truck, freight, etc. of which these options include shipping costs depending on the distance and weight of the products you are shipping.

Imports from other countries are under a government law of "Custom duties and taxes", which suggest that all imports should be examined and taxed before they are released from the Airport or receiving It is required by the government that all imports products from other countries to be examined and accepted in the country and all this process is charged tax and customs fees before products are released to the owner.

7.8. PRODUCTS PRICING

Create a competitive pricing list of your product based on your competition and what type of profit you expect to get. Therefore, determine the retail prices for the customized products by taking the wholesale cost and applying the industry standard mark-up. The industry-standard markup for products is 100%. For the company's retail barbering products, a set price for each will be determined that is inclusive of direct costs and desired profit. The wholesale prices for these products are within industry norms and allow the company to attain projected profit levels. An opportunity to expand offered products exists as FHP has a wide selection of products.

7.9. PRODUCTS TIMING

Releasing your products to the open market requires a proper analysis of the right time. When you do the right thing at the wrong time, you don't get rewarded, but you reap pain and frustration. Releasing your product too early or too late is risking getting the desired response from the market. For example, releasing the product early means that your product is not providing the solution to the need of the current market is proposing then your product will face a battle. Be sure that your product is providing a solution to a need, more especially a pressing need in the market. Releasing a product too late means the solution your product is presenting has already been already satisfied within the market by other businesses and they have gained mass audience and momentum. Product timing is the right identification of the balance between the supply and demand. So, for you to know when it is the right time to release your product to the market, is when the current need of the market has not yet a product that provides the solution, then that the right time to be the hero and not wait for the courageous to step up and step forward but go ahead release your solution to the need in the market. That's the right product timing.

7.10. PRODUCT DISTRIBUTION

The distribution of your product is the ways or channels you intend to use to get your product to the target market. Distribution is also the expansion strategy of the product; how far do you intend your product to reach. There are stores, platforms, you can utilize to sell your products. Below is the list of distribution methods you can use to expand your product and reach millions of people.

- Selling your product physically in your shop.
- Selling your product online on your shop website.
- Selling your product on eCommerce platforms like Amazon, eBay, Shopify, Takealot, etc.
- Becoming a supplier to stores that sell products.
- Partner with small businesses to sell your product.

CONCLUSION

At the end of reading and applying the knowledge provided in this book you should be able create your own brand barbershop business, able to earn you a good living and make your dreams come true. Barbering education has not been made this easy, this book is a manual for success in your journey of barbering career. For practical classes, we have an institution called, "BCC Academy" which is an accredited barbering training center in south Africa, we provide outstanding quality training and education which is NQF and SAQA aligned. Our course takes a duration of two weeks, both practical and theory classes with our certified and professional barbers as teachers.

Our mission is to produce high quality professionals in the barbering industry. Our training is focused on all areas pertaining to barbering and business management. We are also accredited trade test center for barbering. We host barber trade shows, seminars, and events. Do kindly visit our website to get more info about us:

Contact:
Tell: +(27)12-065-4239
Email: info@bcc-academy.co.za
Website: https://www.bcc-academy.co.za/
Social Media:
WhatsApp: +(27)73-972-5319
Facebook: BCC Academy SA
Instagram: bcc academy sa

We wish you all the best with your barbering career. We would love to hear from you soon. THANK YOU!!

www.ingramcontent.com/pod-product-compliance
Lightning Source LLC
Chambersburg PA
CBHW060539100426
42742CB00013B/2394